If You Give An Elephant Edibles

Again for Ariel & Sam
-S.M.

For Aurora & Celeste
-M.O.

Special Thanks To:
Tosca Miserendino
Stacie Odum
Jack W. Perry
Jesse McHugh
Don Loudon
Ron Riffle
Travis Bundy
Shawn Gates
Beverly Miserendino

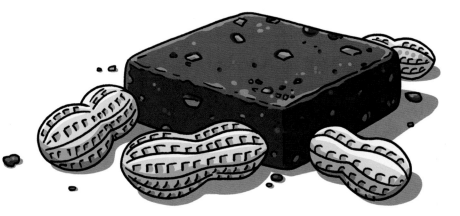

If You Give An Elephant Edibles

Written By Sam Miserendino

Illustrated By Mike Odum

Skyhorse Publishing, Inc.

If you give an elephant edibles,

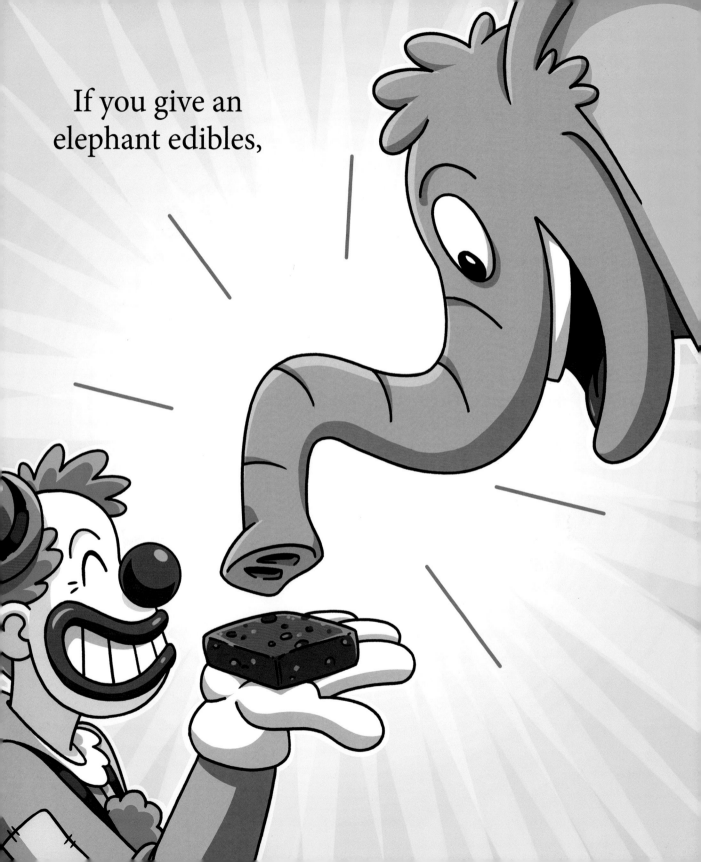

he'll wait for something
to happen.

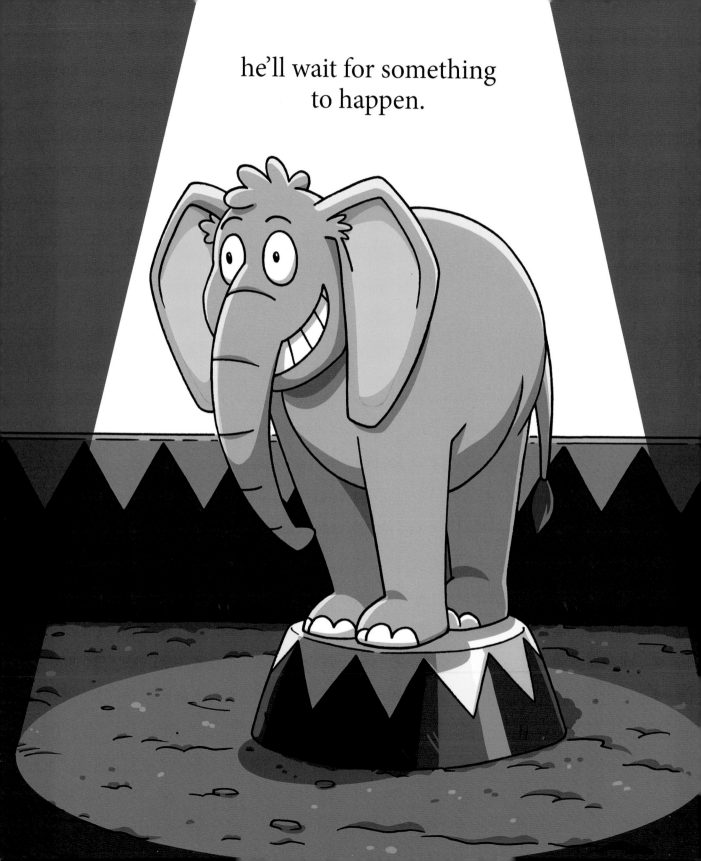

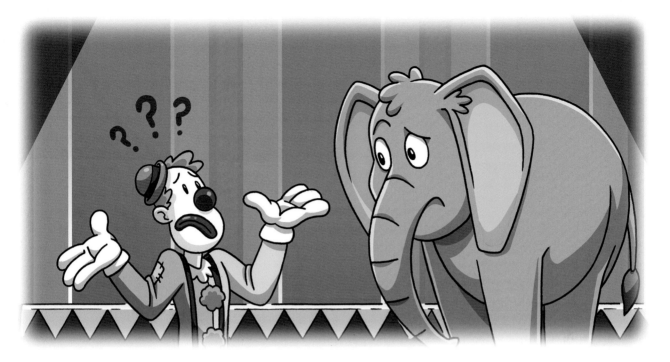

And he'll wait and wait and wait…

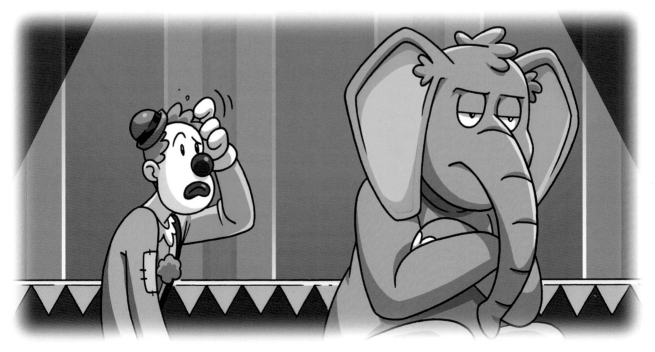

When nothing happens,

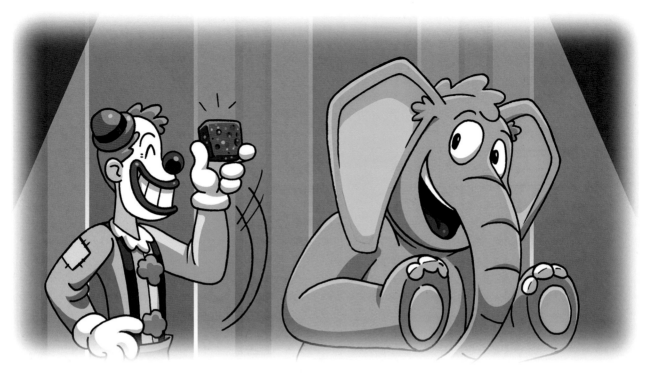

he'll take another...

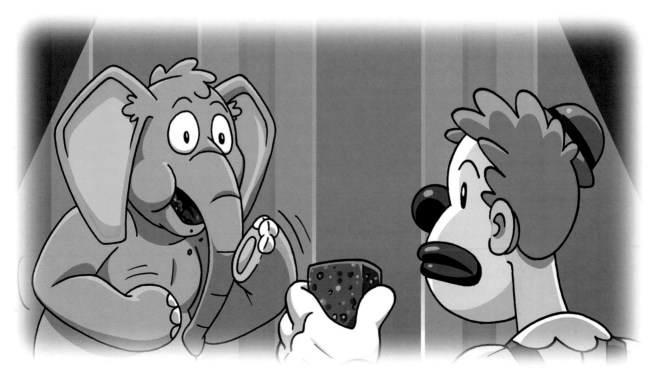

And another...

And another...

THEN...

nothing will happen...

Until it does!

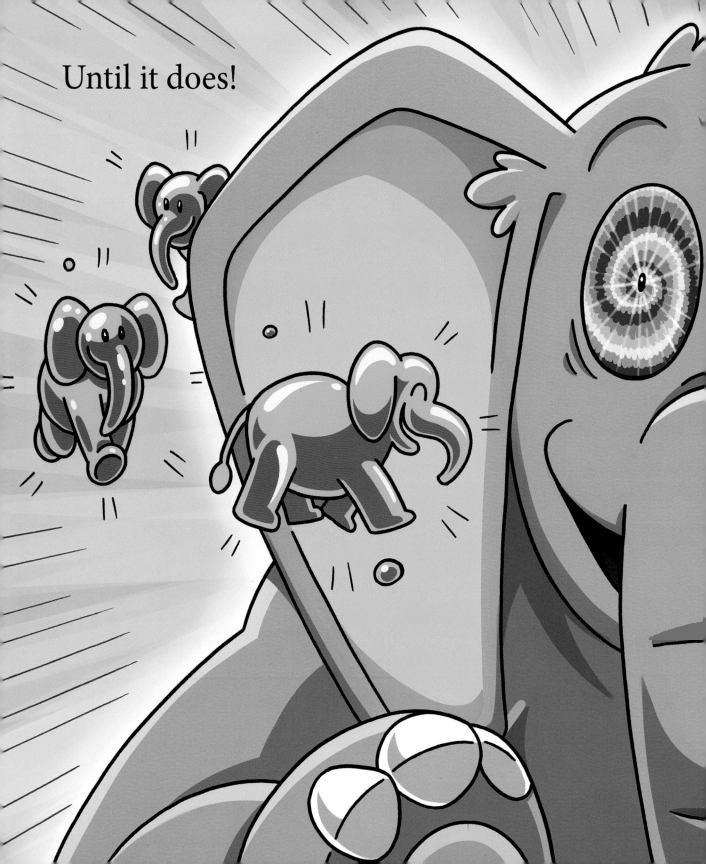

When he steps off
of his stool,

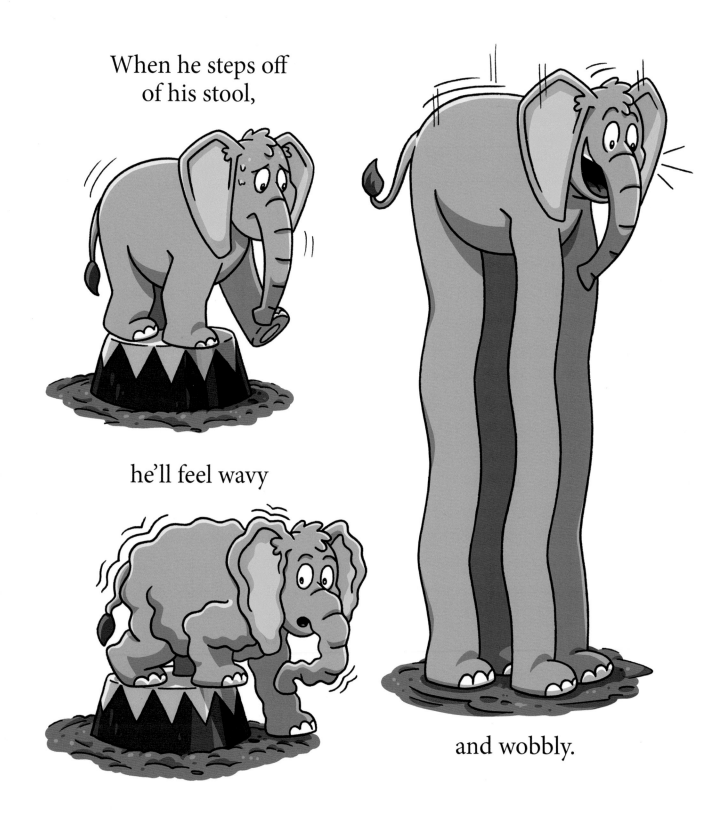

he'll feel wavy

and wobbly.

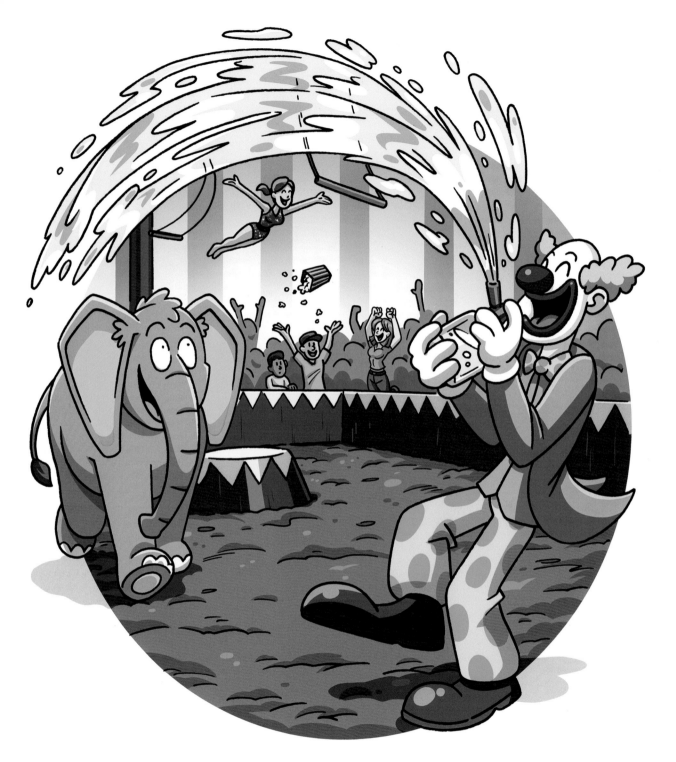

And then, he'll feel like time is
moving very, very slowly...

but it's not.

When he joins
the line,

he will feel like he
is one with the other
elephants...

but he's not.

When you tell him to get up,

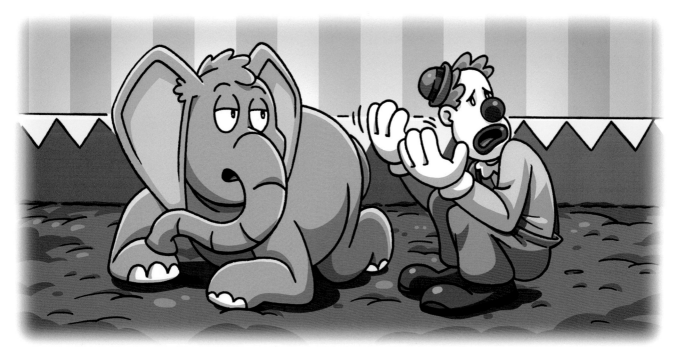

he'll tell you okay, but only...

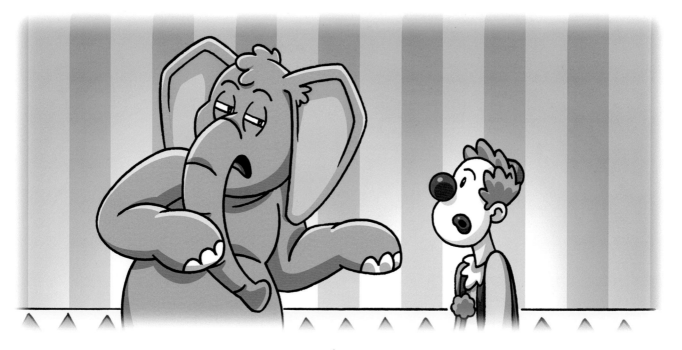

only...

because that peanut over there is calling to him like no peanut ever has before.

And once he's
had one,

he'll want another...

Fresh
EANUTS

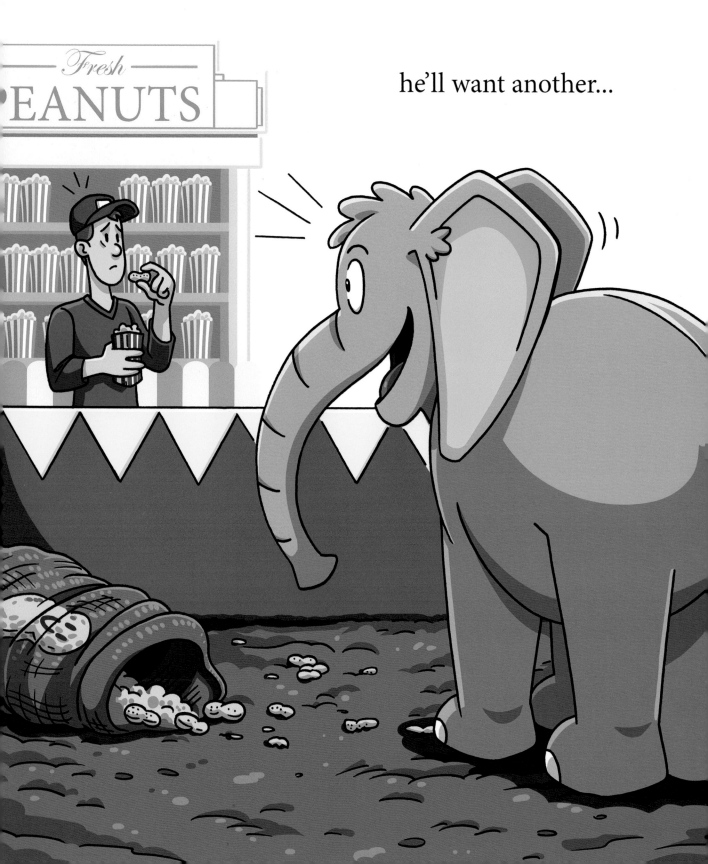

And another...
And another...

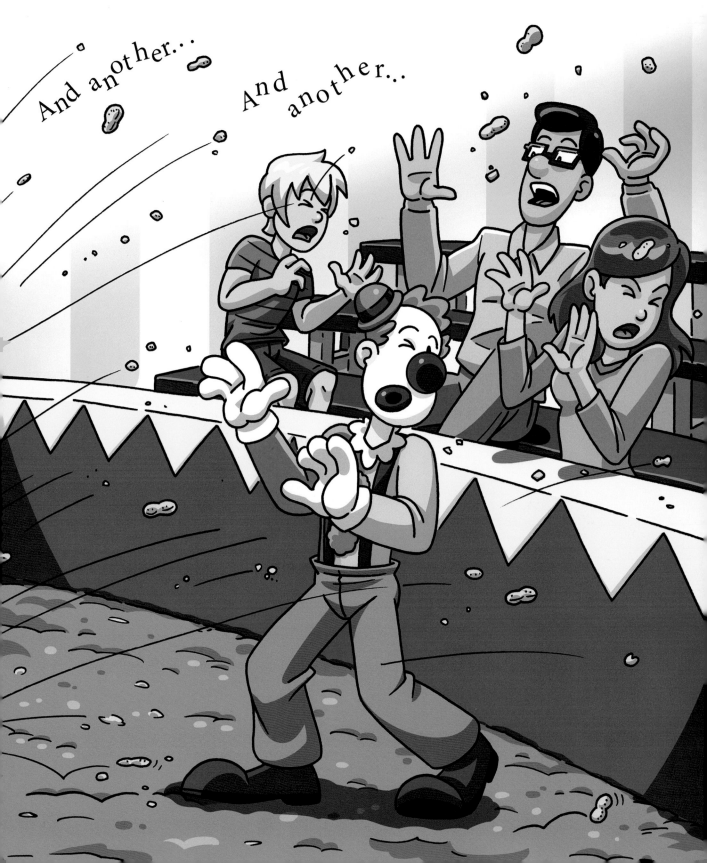

The peanuts will make
him very thirsty, so he'll ask
you for some water...

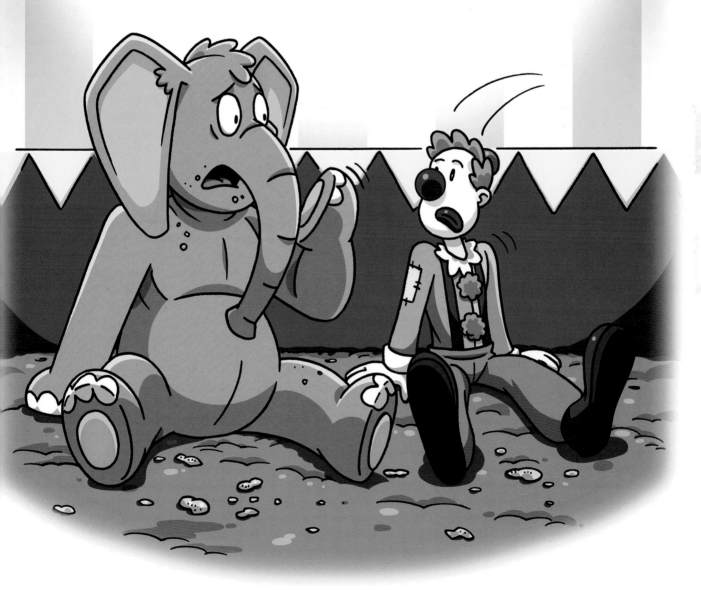

lots and lots of water.

And then,

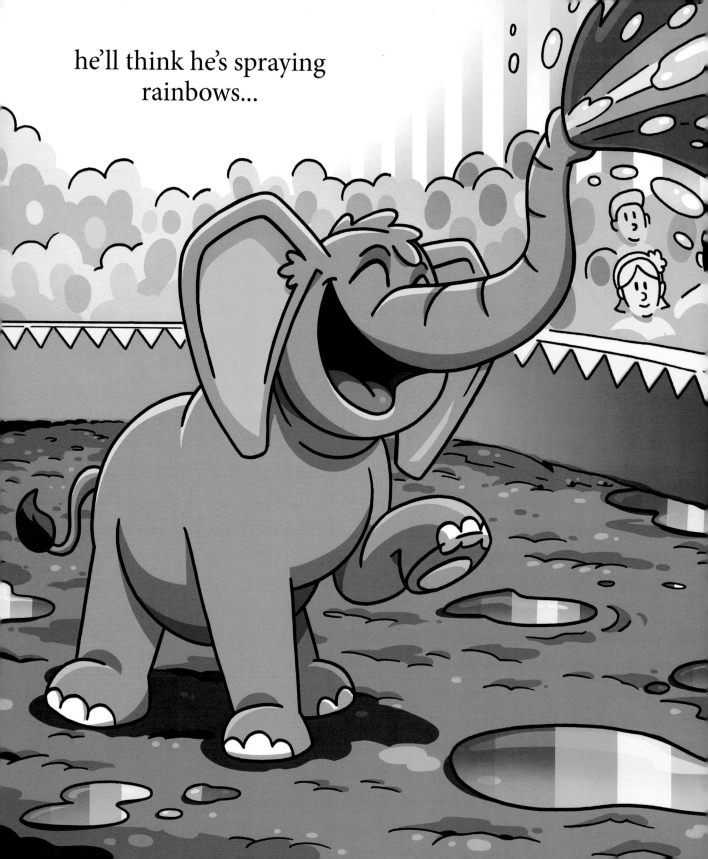

he'll think he's spraying rainbows...

but he's not.

He'll say you probably didn't know
that wet elephants shrink.

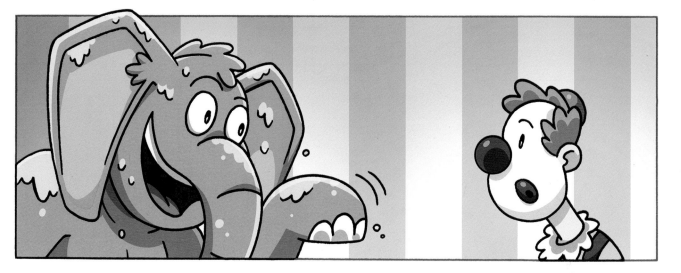

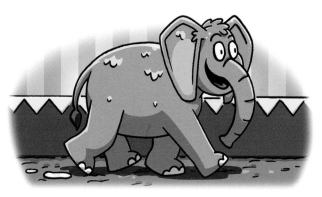

Then, he'll start to feel smaller…

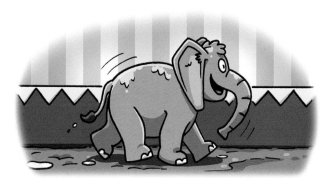

and smaller...

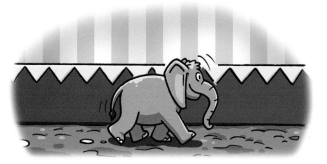

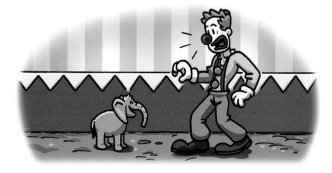

and smaller...

Until he feels
so small,

he'll be absolutely positive he can make it through that hoop...

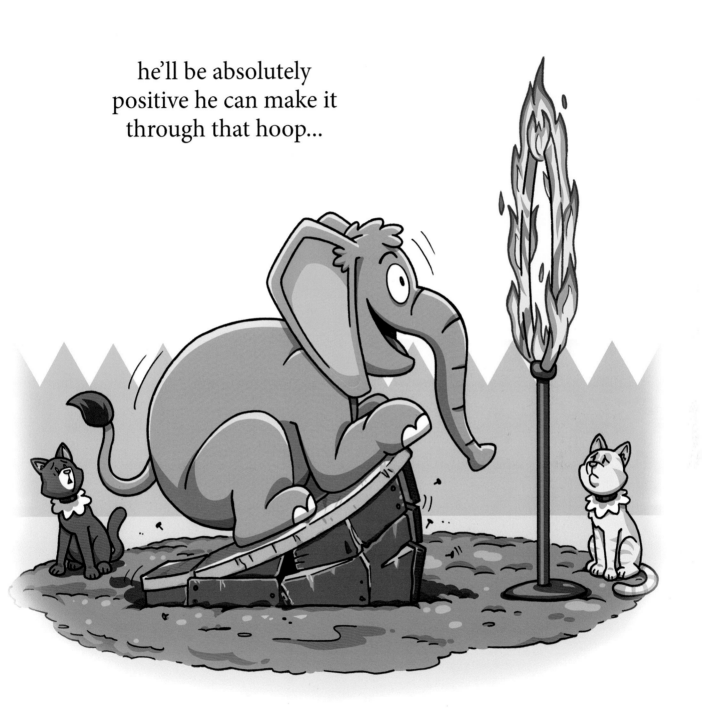

but he can't.

Another thing he'll
bet you didn't know
about elephants,

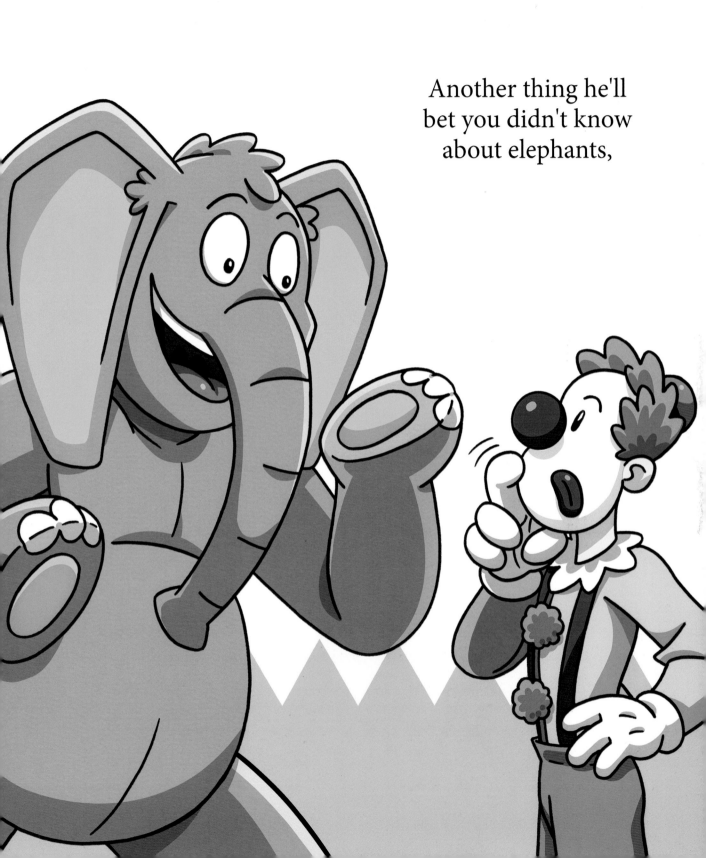

is that an elephant
never, ever...uh...
forgives? Foregoes?

....oh, something
or other.

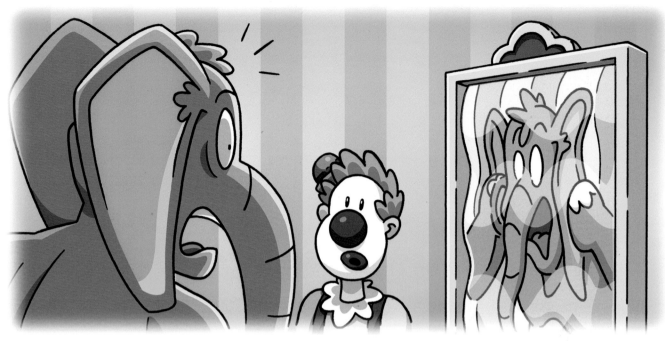

When he suddenly looks afraid, you'll
ask him what's wrong.

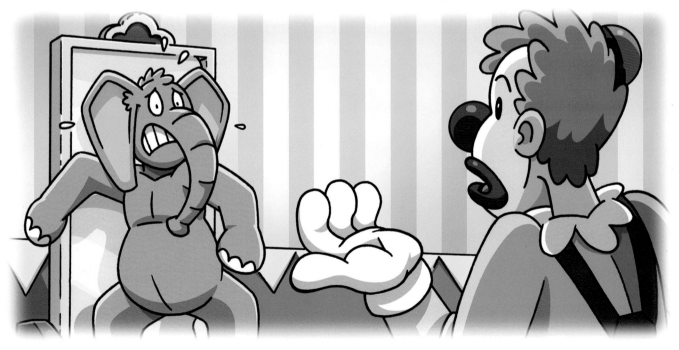

He'll tell you whatever you do, don't
look in the mirror

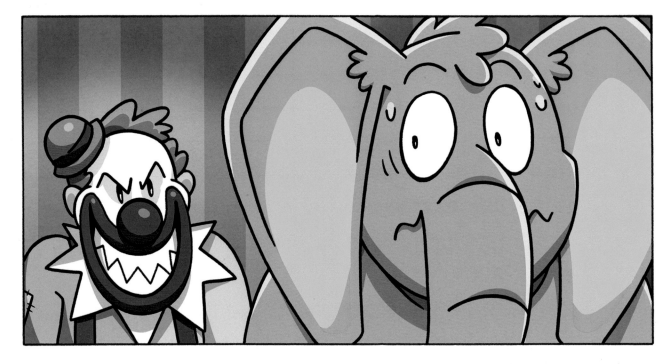

because your face has gotten scary...

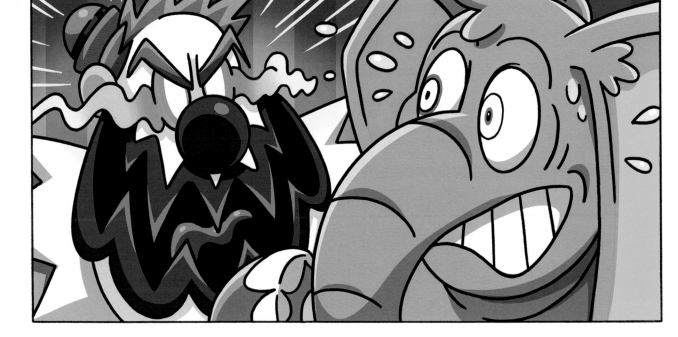

very, very scary!

When you see how
frightened he is,

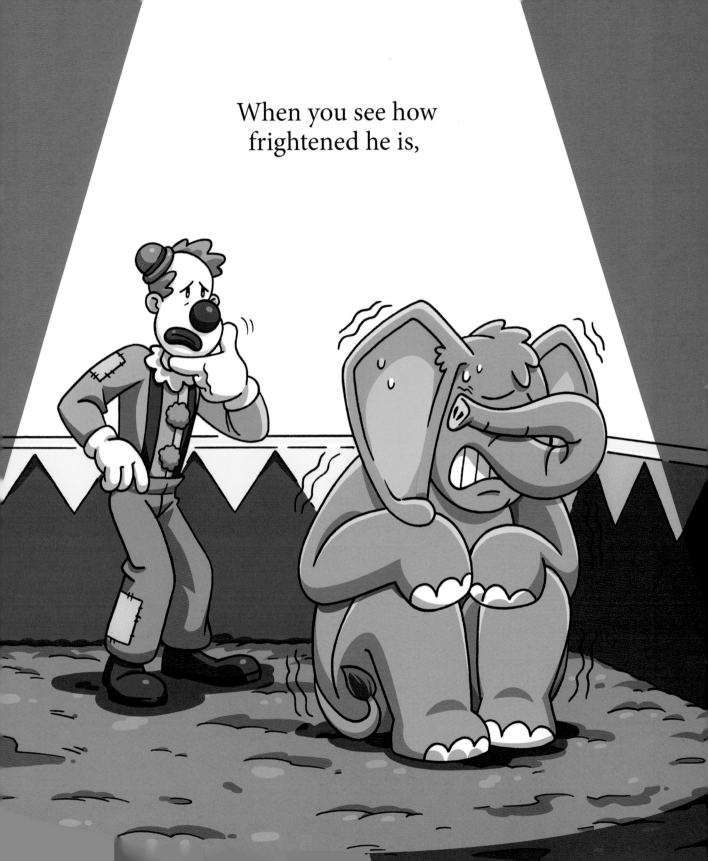

you'll play music to make
him feel better.

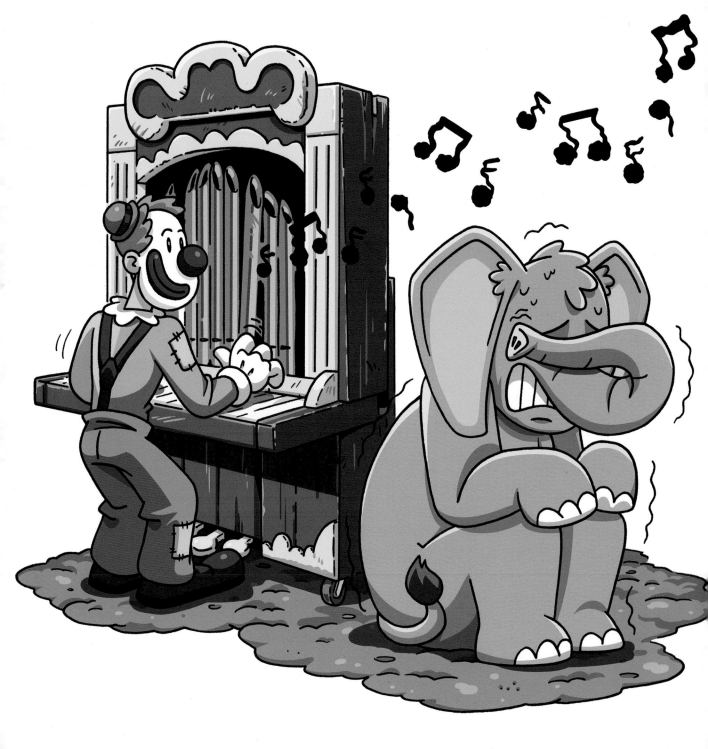

It will be the most amazing
music he's ever heard

and he'll feel like
he's flying...

but he's not!
FLAP
FLAP

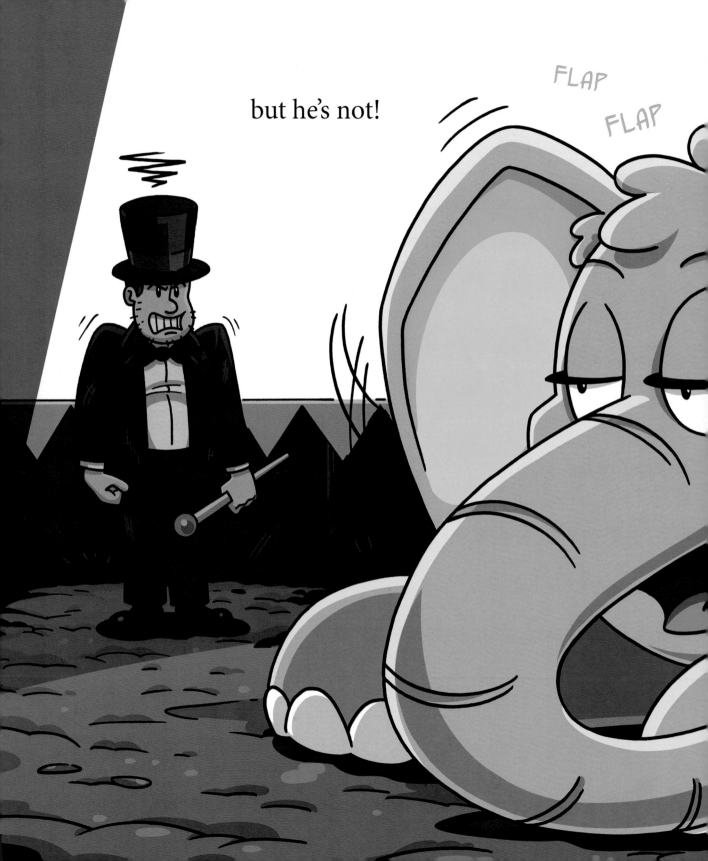

FLAP
FLAP

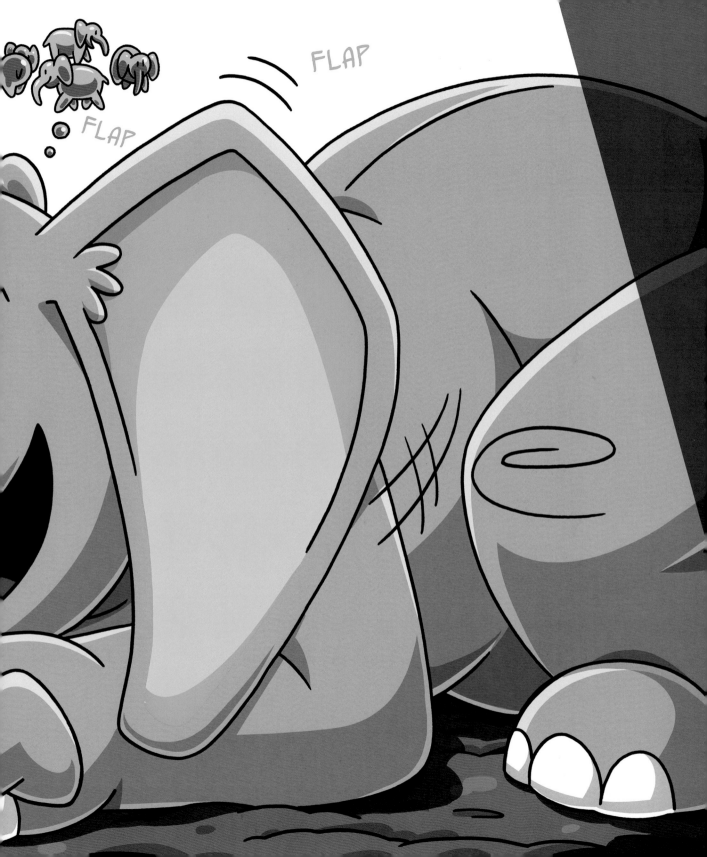

When the edibles
wear off,

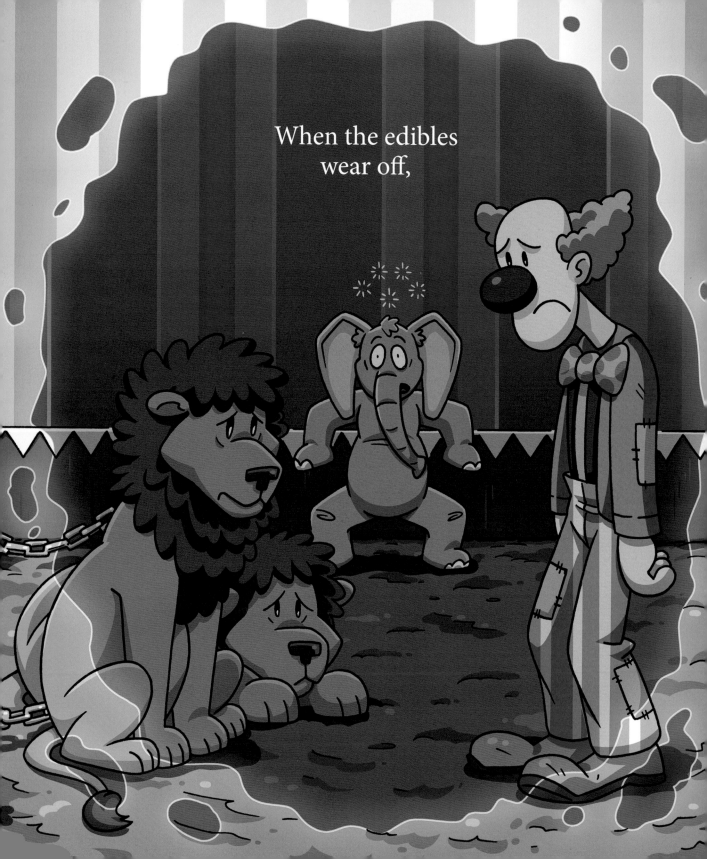

he'll ask you
for more.

When you tell him you don't have any,

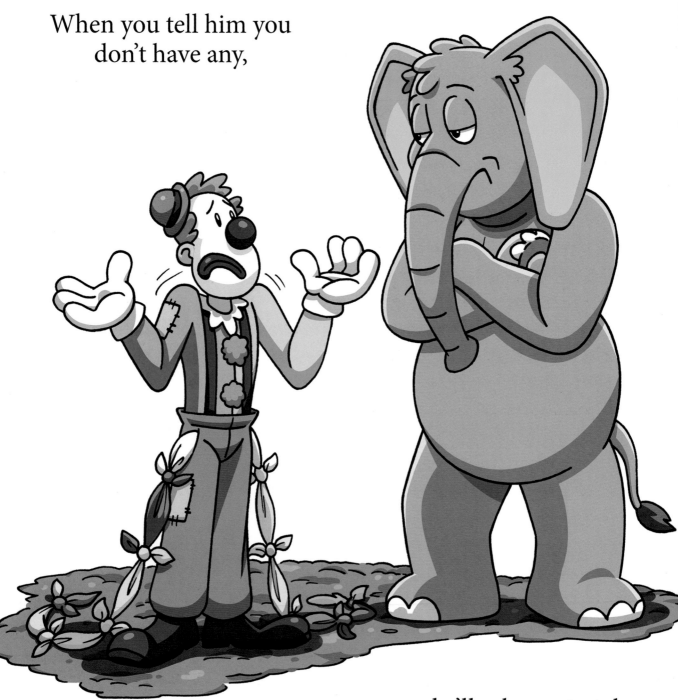

he'll ask you to take him to get some.

Bunny will want
to drive

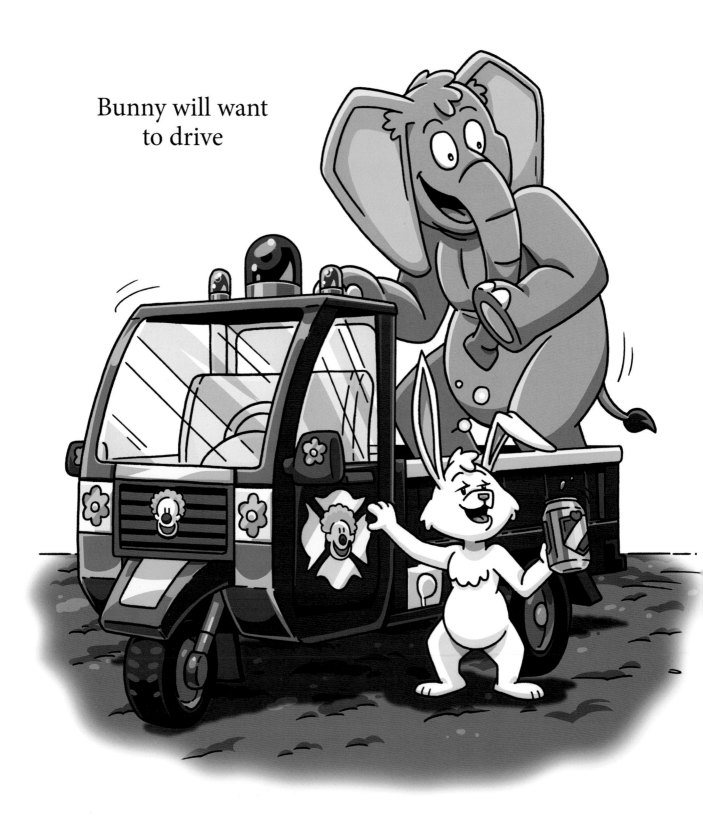

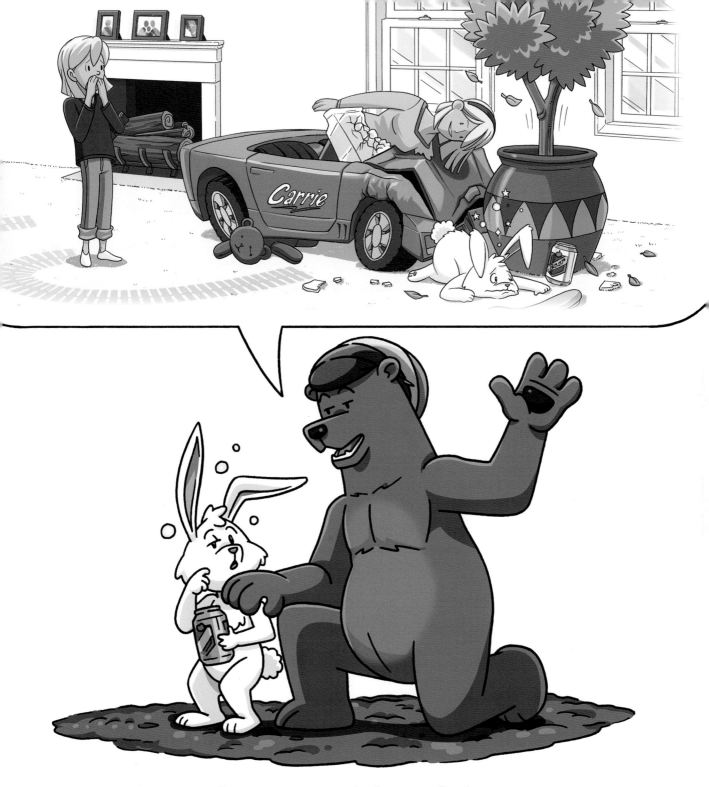

until Bear reminds him of what
happened last time.

So, you'll drive instead.

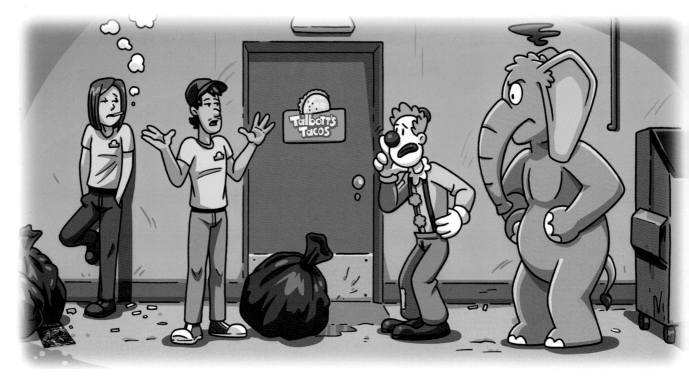

You will take him to the very best places to find edibles...

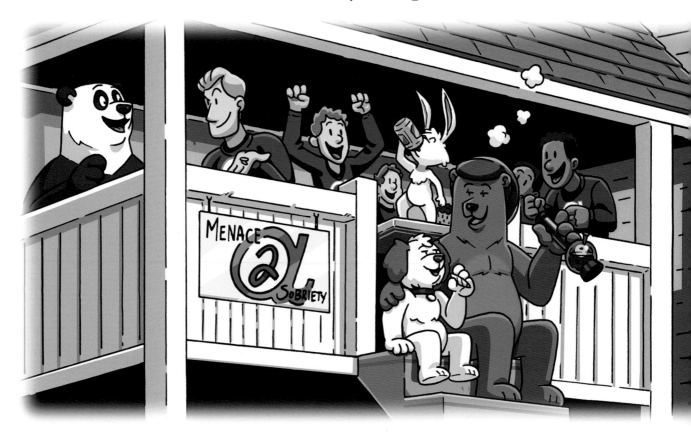

When that doesn't work, you'll drive him to the nearest dispensary.

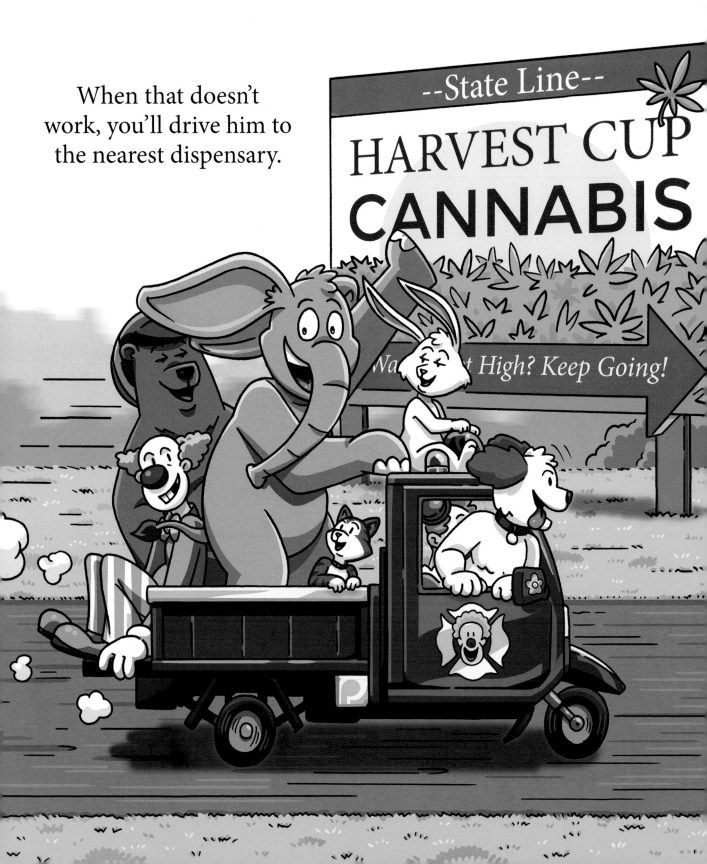

HARVEST CUP
CANNABIS
No Elephants
Allowed!
OPEN

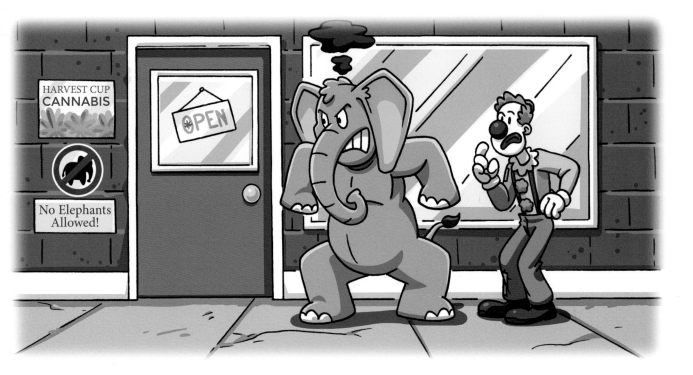

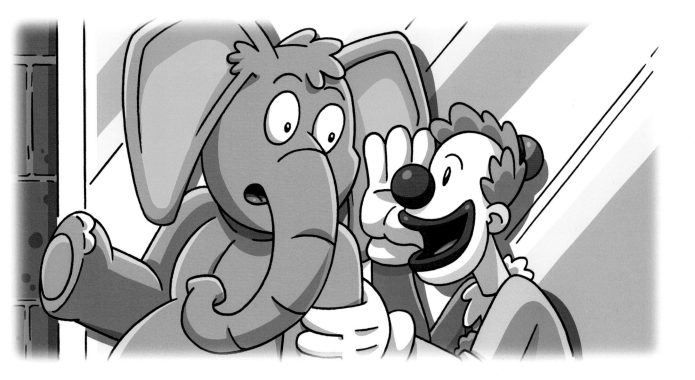

HARVEST CUP
CANNABIS
BROWNIES
SALE!

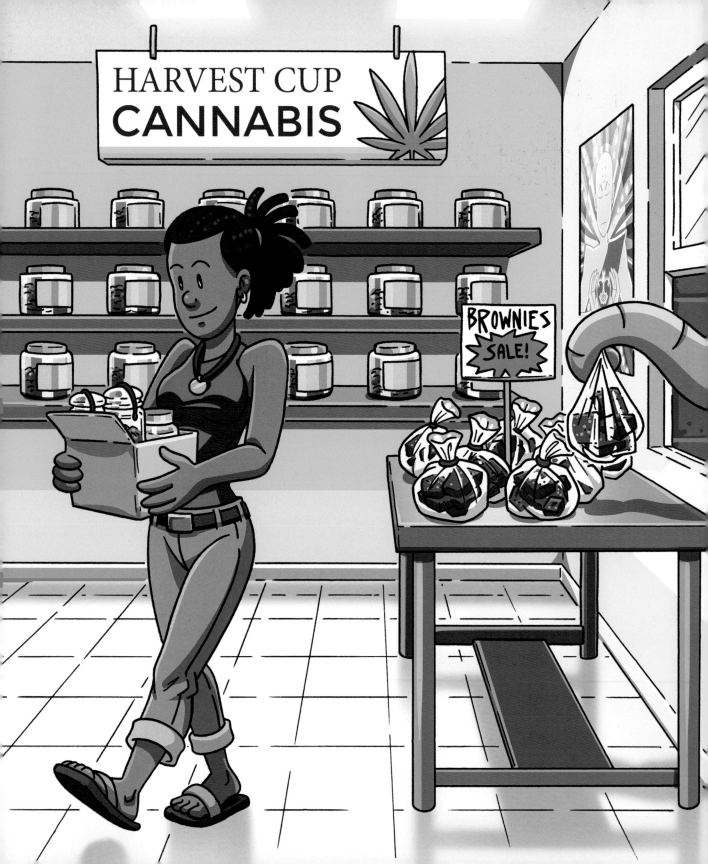

When he gets back
to the circus

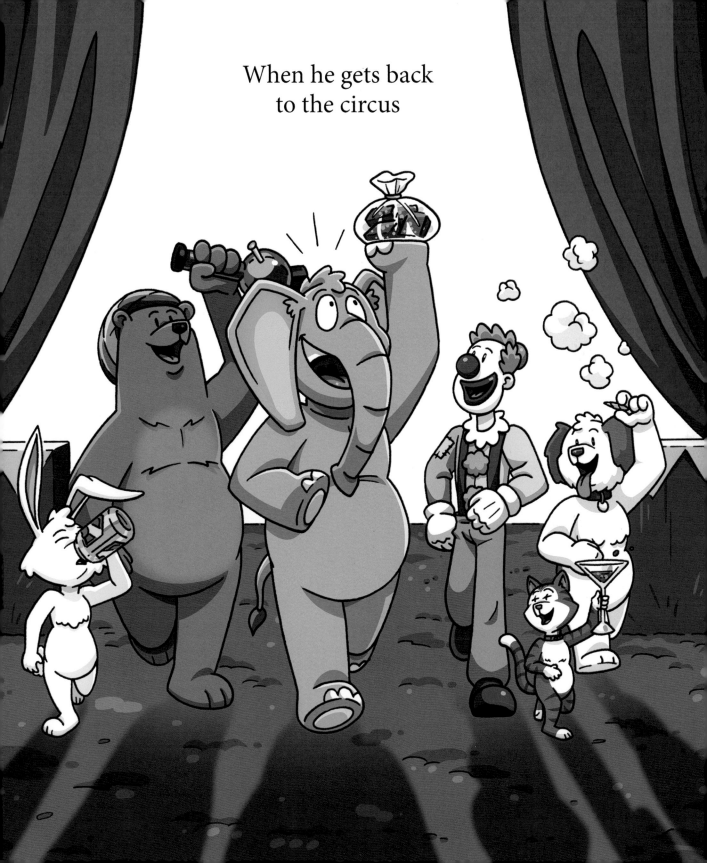

and remember
how much fun
he had,

he'll want to share with
his friends.

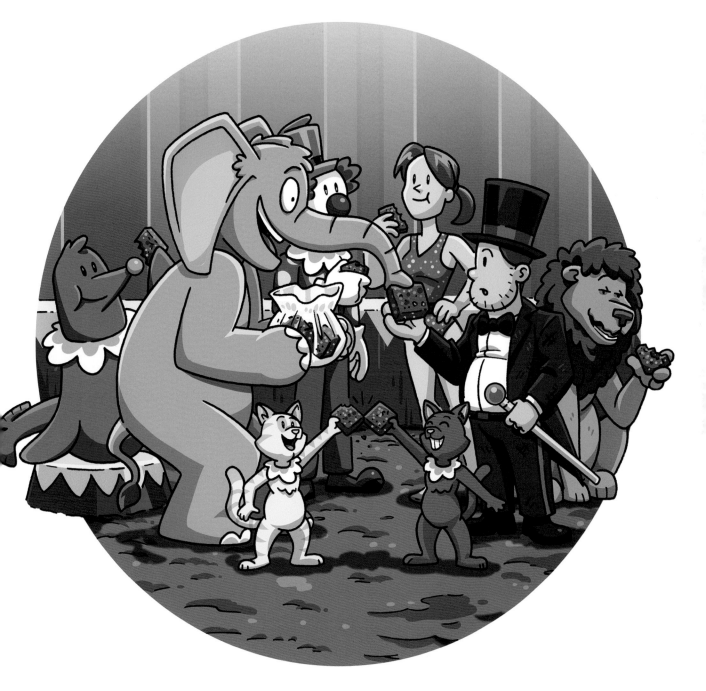

And then,

they'll think they're putting on the most amazing show ever...

But they're not!

THE END

No elephants were harmed in the making of this book. One did, however, have a very good time.